FEEL FREE TO QUOTE ME

365 days of social commentary,
serial commas, and cursing.

The Captain

For Ashley.

JANUARY 1

When I was a kid, and my teachers told
me I could be whatever I wanted to be,
I don't think drunk is what they intended.

I went to Florida once; it was like
being forced to cuddle with someone's
sweaty grandma on a waterbed. Why
the fuck would anybody live there?

I'm sure when Alexander Graham
Bell patented the phone, he was like,
"In 140 years, this will be great for
sending women pictures of your dick."

Aliens haven't contacted Earth
for fear of saying the wrong thing.
You know, since humans are now
offended by basically everything.

Why is it easier to communicate with the dead via Ouija board than it is to communicate with the living via text? Stop ignoring your friends, you fucking dicks.

Maybe she's not answering your texts because she's busy with more important things — like texting guys who don't tYp3 liK di$.

If your boyfriend says you wear too much makeup, paint your face like a circus clown. Leave it until he stops complaining about stupid shit.

I'm not racist, I love all races.
Except marathons. Fuck running.

Turtlenecks are just sweaters
that haven't been circumcised.

Couples that share a Facebook
account are like couples that share a
toothbrush — you're fucking disgusting
and I hope your relationship fails.

Patience is waiting for your friends without losing your mind. Progress is learning that your friends are always late, so you tell them to show up at 7 instead of 8.

Dating is like chewing gum: it's always better if your friends didn't have it first.

If you're still grossed out by periods, you need to grow the fuck up. That should be the least of your hole concerns; the shit that comes out of some people's mouths is far more disconcerting.

When I was a kid, I wanted to be a cowboy. Then, I realized it wasn't 1842, so I asked my mom for a skateboard and got on with my life.

Remember when kids wanted to be firemen, lawyers, and doctors; instead of DJs, models, and pregnant food bloggers? Man, those were the days.

Political Opinions: Giving you new
reasons to hate your friends since 1788.

The easiest way to break it off with a girl is to tell her she kisses like your sister. Girls hate it when you compare them to your family.

A picture really is worth a thousand words, but sometimes those words are just "fuck you" written over and over again five hundred times.

I'd smash my own face with an axe long
before I'd ever put another human's toe
in my mouth — you people are sick.

Think of your life like a big-ass Etch-A-Sketch: if you don't occasionally shake things up, your picture will always be the same.

All dogs go to heaven, except Poodles.
Those dogs are assholes.

You can be pretty, but with a bad personality you're just a sticky stack of porno mags. Good for passing time, but nothing to tell Mom about.

Sure, you can grab the bull by the horns, but you'll probably die. I mean, have you seen a bull? Those things will totally fucking kill you.

Admit it, if you ever get murdered,
you want your killer to be attractive.
Nobody wants the last face they see to
be anything less than an 8 out of 10.

Anybody who says, "You can't judge a book by its cover," in reference to themselves, should be forced to write an autobiography to prove it.

It can take years to build a reputation,
and just minutes to destroy one.
Think about that the next time you
consider buying Skechers.

A life without goals is like a dog without balls. You can hump and grind all you want, but you won't leave anything behind when you die.

Throwback Thursday is cool
because you get to see how ugly
some people were as kids.

If you like someone, just fucking tell them. Playing it cool all the time is a great way to ensure you'll be playing with yourself most of the time.

You'd probably have more friends if
you used complete sentences instead
of hashtags to describe your feelings.

Telling someone, "I miss you," is admitting you're a boring person when you're alone. Get a fucking hobby.

Ignorance is only bliss if the ignorant keep to themselves.

Being a mom is easy: feed your kids, don't smoke crack, give them normal names, and let them be as weird as they want when they grow up.

Few things are more attractive than someone who's not afraid to speak their mind. Aside from bonding over the mutual things we hate, the best dates involve a good debate.

The coolest part of being a vampire
would definitely be the immortality.
You could procrastinate simple tasks
for fucking decades.

Don't wear a tiara on your birthday.
You're not a fucking princess.
You're a drunk, 26-year-old,
beauty school dropout.

Be yourself, do you, enjoy YOUR life —
but don't ask me to participate in "Dry
January" with you. Because, personally,
I think that's fucking ridiculous.

Oh, you want to travel the world?
Cool. Start with the middle of the
ocean, we're all sick of your shit.

Turns out, if you turn off your phone
every once in a while, you might actually
notice someone in real life paying
attention to you.

Pizza consumption should be like sex:
No forks, no napkins, and no excuses.
Followed by immediate regret.

Unless your job title ends with 007, there's no reason to have a private profile. Nobody's life is that mysterious and interesting.

"I have a private profile because of my crazy ex." Don't lie to yourself, it's private because you're boring and your pets are shy.

I just want a girl who swears like
a sailor, dresses like a lady, and
cares like a bear.

I love any girl who knows the
difference between "you're" and "your,"
but doesn't bother correcting people
because she's better than that.

VALENTINE'S DAY

Love is in the air today;
hold your fucking breath.

Dating a crazy girl is like flying on an airplane: It's fast-paced and adventurous — but if something goes wrong — you'll probably fucking die.

When someone refers to themself as,
"a hopeless romantic," it really means
they're an unrealistic, undateable,
needy-fucking-crazy person.

I respect polyamorous relationships.
These people are out here loving
two, three, or even four different
individuals — while most people
can't even fucking love themselves.

I want the kind of girl who's great at hiding her emotions, but would be even better at hiding a body. You know, someone I can depend on.

The only problem with free speech
is that it's not often preceded by
intelligent thought.

Liking your own Instagram posts is no different than a dog licking his own balls. Just because you can do it, doesn't mean you should.

Always dress nice for a first date with someone you met online. Because if you go missing, that becomes your "last seen wearing" outfit on the news.

I enjoy being slightly hungover.
The severe dehydration really
brings out the definition in my abs.

I think the worst part of being blind
would be trusting others to dress
you. What if you're walking around
in Skechers like a fucking idiot?

It's almost Friday, you better text back all the friends you've ignored during the week so you'll have something to do.

Life is a series of mistakes, mishaps, and misfortunes that will stress you the fuck out. Followed by the search for cool humans, hobbies, and happy hours to help you mellow out.

A filter can hide a bad nose job, but you'll never find a filter to hide the fact that your boyfriend has no job.

Dating Tip: Any dude wearing a polo shirt has a nickname for his dick. And any dude with a pet name for his privates, is already in a relationship with himself.

I hope there's WiFi in space.
Because I guarantee you at least
one astronaut has tried sending his
girlfriend a zero-gravity dick pic.

A "jury of your peers" doesn't exist.
If they were really your peers,
they'd be on trial with you.

Don't follow the crowd if you actually
want to go somewhere in life, because
you know where the crowd goes:
Walmart. Fucking Walmart.

Anyone who says they miss
high school has obviously
become a loser as an adult.

Most people are like dumpsters on
fire: From far away, the flames look
warm and inviting, but up close,
they're just a burning pile of shit.

Don't waste time telling someone
why you're better than their ex;
use a semicolon correctly and
SHOW THEM why you're better.

People think it's weird I'm single;
I think it's weird you sleep
wearing socks. End of story.

Your spirit animal doesn't give a fuck
about being your spirit animal. And,
that's what makes it so damn cool. In
other words — instead of finding animals
to look up to — try not giving a fuck
about what others think of you.

Oh, your girlfriend is your "WCW"
for the 27th week in a row?
Didn't see that coming.

"If traveling were free, you'd never see me again." Good. How do we make that happen? We'd all love to see you disappear forever.

Never hang out with anybody who
uses the term, "Thirsty Thursday."
Because they're either underage,
in a frat, or just a fucking douche.

Stop complaining — being an adult
is easy: pay your bills, don't smoke
meth, keep a few close friends, wear
deodorant, and tip your bartender.

Anybody who says, "Come to mama,"
or, "Come to daddy," in an attempt to
sound sexy, is creepy as fuck.

Everybody wants to be a savage,
but not everyone is ready to carry
that baggage. It's fucking heavy
being heady.

Your sensitivity is like an STD:
It's your problem — not mine.

I wish I grew up in the Old West, back when you could shoot someone dead at high noon just for lying to you. All of my friends would be goners.

Following your heart is like closing
your eyes while driving.

ST. PATRICK'S DAY

St. Patrick's Day is the same as every day:
If he has a nice car and a pot of gold, dumb,
materialistic girls will totally fuck a guy
who looks like a leprechaun.

Referring to yourself as a "trophy wife"
doesn't mean much — especially if
you're one of those trophies everyone
gets just for participating.

They say imitation is the sincerest form of flattery. I say imitation is the easiest way to no longer be friends with me.

You know what's cool about spring?
Everyone pretends they like hiking.

I want a woman with a foul mouth who can chew her way through a fucking tent like a bear — and look damn good doing it.

Sober friends only care about two things: their bedtime and their battery life.

Girls only like beards because
they like bread and all other
carbohydrates, and the word "beard"
is just "bread" spelled incorrectly.

Old people are rad: driving all
shitty, dressing like cartoons,
taking drugs because they actually
need them to live — ha, classic.

I'm not going to lie, whenever I
see a couple with matching outfits,
I immediately start clearing space
in my trunk for two bodies.

Body language is cool because it's
like, "Hey, I need to tell you something,
but I can already tell that talking to
you is a waste of breath."

If you think it's clever to use an emoji or the word "donut" in place of the words "do not": First of all, it's spelled d-o-u-g-h-n-u-t. Secondly, doughnut fucking text me with that dumb shit.

When I die, I want a barbershop quartet to sing "Happy Birthday" at my funeral; I want to ruin the feeling of that song for everyone.

Dating is like buying a lottery ticket:
It's a waste of money and you'll
probably lose — and if you do win —
all your friends will hate you.

I want a girl who's stubborn,
independent, AND humble. Like, she'll
cut her own hair just to prove you
wrong, but will admit it was a mistake.

I bet the first guy to get drunk was like, "Fuck, I've been poisoned — I'm gonna die." Then, woke up wishing he had died when he saw who he slept with.

APRIL FOOLS' DAY

April 1st is the same as every day:
You still can't believe 95% of what
you read online, your friends are still
full of shit, and 2Pac is still dead.

If you think your boyfriend is cheating, burn his fucking house down. See who he chooses to move in with when he has nowhere to go.

Non-drinkers will never understand the magnitude of the terms "free drinks" or "open bar." It's like hearing, "Welcome to heaven."

You can pretty much carry anything
in cargo shorts — except your dignity.
You sacrifice self-respect for an extra
pocket of ChapStick and gum.

People are like plastic bags:
Some are meant to fly, some have
holes (but are still useful), and, well,
others are full of dog shit.

Don't get me wrong, Axe body spray
is great if you're trying to pass for
someone underage.

If your life is a mess, just walk away.
Because if there's one thing movies
have taught us: You look badass
walking away from explosions.

Sure, there are plenty of fish in the sea, but you still need good bait to catch one. And your bait — a.k.a. your personality — is fucking garbage.

You're not an emotional rollercoaster, rollercoasters go up AND down. You're an emotional waterslide — you cry too much and you only go down.

If you want to date someone "spontaneous," date someone bipolar. Better yet, date a fucking schizophrenic.

I want a girl who doesn't give up. Like,
just when you think the relationship
is finally over... BAM! She's crawling
through your fucking window.

You should respect your parents. At your age, they actually had their shit together. They didn't just Google how to fucking do everything.

I want a girl with nice teeth and
ambition. You know, a girl not afraid
to bite off more than she can chew.
I want a shark, not a mermaid.

Maybe your dog always tries to run out the door because he's late for a meeting. Ever think about that? You don't know what he does all day.

Since when is a drinking problem
not tax-deductible? Do you have any
idea how much money I pump into
the local economy?

Turns out Tinder is a lot like Netflix:
Full of options, but 98% of them are
fucking garbage. And anything good,
you saw five years ago.

Don't let anybody kill your dreams. If
Dr. Phil can pretend to be a doctor, you
sure as shit can pretend to be attractive.

Talking about your diet is like participating in a flash mob: It's a big deal to you, but to everybody else, it's fucking annoying.

I hate when people don't follow leash
laws. If you're going to have kids,
control them in public.

4/20

4/20 reminds me of high school.
Because all of my friends posting
about it still have the same job
they had in high school.

Safe sex is asking someone to brush
their teeth before they go down —
nobody wants plaque on their privates.

Instead of thinking about all the
things you'd buy if you were rich,
think about all the people you could
pay to never talk to you again.

The best accessory a girl can wear is not a smile — it's a house arrest ankle monitor. She's fun, and a homebody.

Fake boobs, fake eyelashes, fake hair,
or fake gluten allergies. You can't
have all four, choose three.

I want the kind of girl who would
rescue a puppy from a fire, but may
have also started the fire herself.

When I was a kid, if someone pointed out your stupidity, it wasn't called "shaming." We called it what it was: a fucking reality check.

"I'm not here to hook up." Good.
Set realistic goals; you won't be
depressed when nobody talks
to you at the bar tonight.

I'm envious of people who can enjoy hot-ass summer weather without sweating. I suppose once you've dated the Devil you become acclimated to every level of Hell.

Female dragonflies play dead to avoid unwanted male advances. Which makes a lot of sense because not everyone will give you butterflies in your stomach; some will give you dragonflies instead — making you wish you were dead.

Back in the day, when someone said, "adventure," it meant they were going to go Lewis & Clark some shit. Now, they're just going to brunch.

New phones are like new relationships:
They're super fucking confusing at first,
and when you finally get comfortable,
it's time to upgrade.

I know girls think it's cute to brag about how grumpy they are before they have coffee, but honestly, it kind of just means you're a bitch.

Relax, pretty much every mistake you make in life is reversible. Except for murder and crying on National TV.

Casual sex is like washing/drying a fitted sheet: It seems easy enough, but the next thing you know: things get heated, feelings get twisted, and your favorite t-shirt goes fucking missing.

Avoid people who say, "I'm down to earth." They're serial killers, just waiting to cut you up and bury you in the earth they're so "down with."

You know you're a deadbeat when
even the local library will no longer
let you borrow their shit.

If babies are really "little miracles,"
why does everyone at Walmart look
so damn miserable? That place is
fucking crawling with magic.

This Mother's Day, give your mom
something she really wants — like
my phone number. I'll show her
she's appreciated.

Sure, variety is the spice of life —
but self-discipline is the recipe that
will keep you from spicing up your
life with shit like meth, debt, and
unhealthy relationships.

If you go out tonight wearing all black, bring a fanny pack, so you'll have a place to put all the fucking compliments you're gonna get.

Stop dressing your kids like "cool adults" in order to make yourself feel better about your own life. You both look like fucking douchebags.

Girls, if a knight on a white horse tries to save you, tell him to leave and come back with a better horse — a black horse — because black matches your outfit.

Smart girls are hot. Because anybody
can buy boobs, but you actually have
to work to develop brains.

Sometimes I feel like I missed out on my true calling in life. With how often I can successfully convince people I'm "not drunk yet," I really should have pursued a career in acting.

Whenever you feel self-conscious,
remember this: Somewhere, someone,
is confidently wearing blue lipstick
on a first date. If they can do that...

Dating a girl who works out a lot is cool until you realize she can kick your ass. And, will fucking kill you if you eat her peanut butter.

Bars with dress codes are the best.
Because the last thing I want to see
when I'm already trying not to throw
up is some dude in flip-flops.

My favorite part of "Beauty and the Beast" is when he changes from a badass into a dude who looks like he's named Brandon and she still loves him — I cry every time.

Cats suck. If I wanted a confusing, cold-hearted creature living with me, I'd get a girlfriend.

Scientific Fact: Sunglasses make people look more attractive because they add symmetry to an otherwise fucked-up face.

Sometimes I feel bad swearing
around kids, but then I remember kids
these days are desensitized, fucking
shitheads with access to the internet.

Looking to drop some excess weight before summer? Dump your fucking boyfriend. That's at least 150 pounds right there — 200 if he's tall.

Guess what, you can cut your hair
and not desperately seek online
opinions first. It's what adults do —
it's called making your own decisions.

Hey high school girls, dating a guy in college doesn't make you cool. You're dating a fucking loser — that's why he still dates high school girls.

If you wear sunglasses inside, don't ever complain about girls "fooling you" with their makeup. She's hiding a zit, you're hiding half of your fucking face.

I hope your Monday is short. Like your boyfriend, your temper, and the list of friends who would actually attend your wedding.

Leaving your comfort zone is like
entering a haunted house: It's normal to
be scared, it's easier if others are there,
and, in the end, you'll realize that most
of the fear was in your fucking head.

I'd try walking a mile in your shoes,
but I'd rather fucking kill myself than
wear a pair of Skechers.

I don't understand why anybody is against gay marriage. If someone wants to sign their life away and slowly develop hatred for something they once loved — let them.

What's with all these pizza commercials with families ordering only ONE pizza? What kind of fucking family can fill up on that? So fake.

Try something new this weekend.
Like having a conversation with
someone you're not trying to have
sex with. You might learn something.

Some girls complain about being a side chick, yet they take all their advice from Marilyn Monroe — a woman who died a 36-year-old side chick.

Nothing will haunt you more
than a good comeback you
think of 15 minutes too late.

Children are just pets you have to
feed every day. Even weekends.

Here's how you get really good at
something: You fucking suck at it for
a long time, but you keep doing it;
then one day you stop sucking.

The key to remaining creative: Surround yourself with equal amounts of people you love — and people you hate — inspiration comes in all forms.

Whining about going to work on
Monday is like whining about
wearing a condom — shut up and
just be grateful someone is willing
to pay or lay your whiny ass.

As a kid, I never quite understood why anyone would want to fake their own death. As an adult, that's exactly the kind of vacation I'm in the mood for: 3–6 months with a miraculous story of returning from the dead.

April Fools' Day is cool because you
can say whatever the hell you want
to people and just claim it was a joke.
Kind of like every day of the year.

Gross yet true: Alcohol can be used to kill internal parasites. You know, like worms — or those disgusting, nervous butterflies that your crush gives you every time they're around.

I once saw a lady eating corn on the cob while driving, and I gotta say, cobbin' and driving looks sketchy as fuck. We definitely need a law against that.

I want the kind of girl who's into kinky things like blindfolds, but is also into important things, like her 401(k) and breakfast sandwiches.

If you're ever wearing pajamas in public and somebody gives you shit about it, just tell them you're dressing for the job you want. And, when they ask what that is, respond with, "Retired."

Having a black belt in karate basically means you've mastered kicking the shit out of air — not really something to brag about.

When you think about it, making out is pretty fucking weird: "Hey, you're hot, I'm hot — let's touch our food holes together."

I love the mystery of women with aviator sunglasses. They look like they enjoy traveling, but might also crash a fucking plane into my house.

Leg day? Pfffft, every day is leg day.
I fucking walk and stuff.

Oh, so you're staying in tonight
because there's nothing going on?
Trust me, there are TONS of things
going on. You just weren't invited.

Tweet like Marilyn Monroe: "If you can't blow two dudes at once, you're wearing the wrong shade of lipstick."

This Father's Day, give your dad something he really needs — like a break from your shit. Don't call, text, or visit; he's earned a day off.

Oh, you hate Mondays? Let me guess, you also love bacon, NEED coffee, and think you're ugly. What other basic shit are you posting today?

I want the kind of girl who will cook breakfast in the morning, but might also hit me with the frying pan. You know, a lover and a fighter.

The best thing about deleting your Facebook account: You no longer have to buy your friends birthday presents — because you won't even know when their birthday is.

If you steal from other people, you suck. Make your own money, buy your own bike, develop your own style, and write your own fucking tweets.

Why do pregnant ladies have baby showers? Babies don't shower — they take baths. You haven't even had the kid and you're already fucking up.

Ladies, if he has typos on his profile, you're wasting your time. If he can't even proofread his hobbies, he'll never provide for a family.

Marrying your high school sweetheart
is like keeping the same haircut
for your entire life. Trust me, you'll
eventually regret those bangs.

Don't lie to yourself, you're not going to find your soulmate at a bar this weekend. You can't even find matching socks when you're sober.

I want a girl who talks shit to me, but has my back. Like, she'll tell me I'm being stupid — but if someone else does — she'll fucking cut them.

"I'm going to relax, watch two episodes, and go to bed early tonight. I'm going to get so much fucking sleep." ... SIX EPISODES LATER ... "Shit."

If a Kardashian dyeing their hair is really news to you, you need to get some fucking hobbies.

Moms, stop yelling at your kids in public. I get it, you're frustrated, but it's not their fault nobody's buying your stupid crafts on Etsy.

Airport security sucks. If I wanted
someone to boss me around,
ask me stupid questions, and go
through all my shit — I'd be married.

Why would anybody have a wedding
without an open bar? Love without alcohol,
is like a movie without swearing — it's
pretty fucking boring.

THE 4TH OF JULY

Girl, are you a firework? Because
you look pretty unstable; like you're
about ready to blow the fuck up.

I'm super envious of anyone with voices in their head telling them to do crazy shit; the voices in my head only tell me to eat pancakes.

There's nothing wrong with admitting a baby is ugly — they're too young to know you're talking shit about them anyway.

Squat goals and hair goals, but what about your life goals? You know, you can have thick thighs and thick hair, but still have a shit life.

How to tell if a guy likes you: Fake drowning at a pool party. See if he tries to save you, or goes inside to make a sandwich and escape "the noise."

Fuck math, you don't need a "better half."
You graduated, right? So why are you still
practicing fractions? Complete yourself:
Be a whole number and become your
own source of satisfaction.

Be honest with yourself, the only reason you want to be invisible is to either see someone naked or steal things — probably both.

"The Hunger Games" is just a movie about basic camping and survival techniques. It's like watching Jennifer Lawrence earn a merit badge.

Dating a psycho is good for you.
Sleeping next to someone who might
kill you in your sleep, makes you
appreciate simply waking up every day.

Dudes, if you're trying to meet a cool woman,
look for a gal out walking her dog. She's
active, clearly has great taste in animals,
AND she's already prepared to pick up shit
off the street — this is your chance.

Don't get me wrong, karate is great
for people who can't hold a gun,
operate a deadbolt, use a cellphone,
or move to a better neighborhood.

Dudes, I don't care how hot it gets this summer, respect yourself enough to not wear flip-flops. Hide your toes, bros.

Why be a baddie when you can just be a bat? Wear all black, hang with like-minded people, and use your instincts like sonar to avoid dumb shit — like worthless situations, your ex, and people you knew in high school.

Why are people so against an Uber
driver talking to them? It's called
being human. That's what separates
us from animals, you fucking dick.

Don't lie to yourself; you'd be a terrible mom. With how often you drop your phone, you know you'll drop a baby.

Fridays are like moms: We all have one, but some of ours are just better than others.

Don't have plans for the weekend?
Good. Now you know how your
parents felt when you were a baby:
bored and miserable.

Oh, you think cats are better than dogs? Ever seen a blind man cruising through the store with his seeing-eye cat? Didn't fucking think so.

Never date a girl with a huge purse.
Trust me, her life is a fucking mess.
She can't even find her lip gloss —
how will she find time for you?

Joggers are always finding dead
bodies. That's why I don't go running;
I don't want to be the one to tell a kid
I found his dead mom.

Saying, "I don't care about politics," is just another way of saying, "I'm too lazy to understand things."

If a couple has a joint Facebook account, who gets custody of the friends when they divorce?

Don't claim to be independent
unless you've gotten off your
parents' insurance, your family's
phone plan, and your ex's Netflix.

Reading books doesn't make you a
dork — it makes you fucking smart.
Watching nothing but Reality TV?
THAT makes you a fucking dork.

Airport security is such a dick tease.
If you select me for a full pat-down,
there's obviously some chemistry
there, at least finish me off.

Being Bigfoot would totally suck.
You're tall enough for the NBA, but
nobody believes in you, so you'll
never get the chance to ball.

Imagine how incredible of a movie
"Titanic" would be if DiCaprio played
the same character in it as he did in
"What's Eating Gilbert Grape."

What's up with dudes wearing
cologne at the gym? Nobody around
you wants to feel like they're working
out in the backseat of an old Cadillac.

Couples get a day, parents get a day, and sharks get an ENTIRE FUCKING WEEK during the summer. I've never felt so unappreciated as a single, childless human.

I'm tired of girls referring to their periods as, "Shark Week." We get it, you're a bitch, but why do you gotta be giving sharks a bad name?

I decided you can judge someone
with 100% accuracy based solely
on their movie and restaurant
recommendations.

Want to compliment a girl? Tell her you would roll naked across a floor of Legos just to smell her hair. If she doesn't appreciate that...

Misery loves company. Why else do
you think all your married friends
keep asking you when you're going
to settle down and have kids?

Behind every male stripper are the
broken dreams of a football player
that wasn't good enough to go pro,
but still wants an athletic career.

I don't get hangovers from drinking,
I get hangovers from knowing I
wasted a night of my life hanging
out with people I don't even like.

Tinder is a great way to experience the rejection of dating without having to leave the comfort of your home.

So many girls on Instagram would lose followers during a zombie apocalypse. Because zombies follow girls for their brains, not their boobs.

In Hell, every password has to be
entered using your TV remote.

The invention of the alarm clock
is proof the human body is not
meant to wake up early.

Unless your nudes include a shark, don't even bother sending them. Not today, not tomorrow, not this week — it's fucking Shark Week.

Fresh eyes save lives. When you're overwhelmed, take a step back to refocus. Doing this will help you avoid doing something frantic — like cutting your hair and immediately regretting your decision, or cutting a person and ending up in prison.

Girls, if you date a guy shorter than you, always wear heels to remind him he's a little bitch. He'll never leave you; he'll be too afraid.

Think your life is boring? Search the
hashtag "blessed" on Instagram.
Look at all the stupid shit people
think is amazing about theirs.

I haven't been to a doctor in years,
but no one at airport security has
reported seeing any weird lumps
when I'm x-rayed, so I think I'm good.

That girl you can't stop thinking about, isn't thinking about you at all. She has two things on her mind: Netflix and brunch.

Guys are like, "I want a girl who's loyal, stays in, doesn't care about money, and isn't a hoe." Dude, you just described a fucking nun.

I want a romance that takes my
breath away. And by that I mean,
I want a hooker to choke me
within an inch of my life.

Women who use charm and looks to
get ahead in life are fucking smart.
Guys only talk shit because they
think strippers actually like them.

I wish I had kids, just so I could unfollow them. They'd be like, "Dad! Why did you unfollow me?!" "Because you're fucking boring, David."

A long-distance relationship is like dating a cat: You rarely see them, you both do your own thing, but at least you're not completely alone — right?

There are two kinds of people in this world: coffee drinkers and sock puppets.

"Age is just a number — we're so in love." You know what else is a number? Two. The number of months I give your disgusting relationship.

It's nice to have a hot ass, but it's cooler to be honest. Not even the sweetest set of cheeks can distract from verbally shitting every time you speak.

Since everyone insists on calling their crappy recording studio, "The Lab," I'll now be referring to my microwave as, "The Olive Garden."

The worst thing about Monday is
listening to everyone complain about it.

I feel like autocorrect is basically just my mom telling me to stop swearing.

The ocean is full of scary shit, like sharks, and stingrays, and gold-digging women drinking champagne on yachts.

Couples, stop sitting on the same side of the booth. Nobody wants to see your disgusting display of affection. We're trying to fucking eat.

Five words to make sex awkward:
"I learned this in prison."

When I was in high school, if you were ugly — you didn't have filters to help attract friends — you had to develop a fucking personality.

It's Friday night, go out and have some fun. Your mom won't invite me over until you leave.

Hiding a weakness doesn't make you strong; openly admitting and defeating your weakness does. For example: Start by admitting that you're powerless around carbs, then, I don't know, (def)eat an entire fucking cake.

Thinking too much about Monday will destroy your Sunday. Kind of like how thinking too much about bodily fluids will destroy your sex life.

If I offend you, cry me a river. I'll bring snacks and a raft. I will literally float down your tears — eating chips and working on my tan.

They say, "God has a hand in everything." That's cool, as long as he keeps it out of my bag of Doritos.

If I ever use a selfie stick, you have permission to kick me in my selfie dick.

Stop acting like you would survive
a zombie apocalypse — you've
never even been camping.

Saying, "No," when a stranger invites you into their van is fucking rude. I mean, I know it's not a Ferrari, but he's obviously still proud of it.

Of course I want to be a dad someday.
You think I like doing my own chores?

If I ever witness a flash mob in person, I hope I'm standing next to Sarah Palin, so I can borrow her pistol and shoot myself in the face.

If your boyfriend complains you don't post him on Man-Crush Monday, tell him to be patient and wait his turn — on Whiny-Bitch Wednesday.

Long-distance relationships are
fucking weird. You basically have
a pen pal who occasionally allows
you to touch their privates.

To the people who make sure to include the word "taken" in their profile description: We get it, you're proud you have someone. And honestly, with a face like that, you should be.

I want a girl who has her shit
together, but is still fun. Like, her
closet is well-organized, but it looks
like a fucking Halloween store.

I don't play video games. If I wanted to escape reality so bad, I'd have a Facebook account. So I could relive high school every fucking day.

"Trusting your gut" means never apologizing for the shit you say when you're hungry. Your stomach is always right.

When you type "vaping," your phone
wants to autocorrect to "gaping,"
because that's the size of your vagina.
Smoke some real cigarettes.

The deepest circle of Hell is reserved for people who can't take a joke. And while they're down there, I'll be on a date with their mom.

He's lying when he says, "Send me a nude, nobody else will see it," because God sees everything. So that's AT LEAST two dudes. Fucking liar.

"Suspect last seen wearing all black."
So basically what you're saying is,
"The dude looks fucking good."

Unless you're an underage girl —
or a cop online pretending to be an
underage girl — talk like an adult
and stop saying, "Sunday Funday."

Summer is over. You can all stop pretending you're allergic to gluten now.

I mean, that's a good-looking selfie,
but that bathroom is terrible. Have you
ever thought of decorating something
other than your face?

"Fuck this, I'll just be a stripper."
Really? You can barely walk in heels,
what makes you think you can make
money dancing in them?

Guess what, if you spell Monday backwards it's "Yadnom." It has the exact same effect as complaining about it — it doesn't fucking do anything.

Treat others how you want to be
treated — unless you're into weird
shit like choking and name-calling.
Don't do that, strangers hate that shit.

Bad advice is sometimes the best advice, because you learn more from your mistakes. In other words, keep reading your daily horoscope.

Guys, stop whining about your
girlfriend taking too long to get ready.
She looks good. Pray some of her
style rubs off on your cargo shorts.

If a weird dude buys you a drink,
don't act all creeped out and rude.
Just say, "Thank you," and drink it.
Because you're not even that hot.

Don't text, "Good morning, beautiful,"
to a girl you just barely met the night
before. You're not smooth — you're
fucking weird and clingy.

I like dating girls with lots of tattoos.
Because they understand pain and
regret; basically the feelings you'll
have after a date with me.

Cardio sucks. Running is meant for survival, not enjoyment. Running is a skill, we as humans, developed to escape scary shit — like dinosaurs and marriage.

If beauty is in the eye of the beholder, what's in the eye of the beauty being beheld? Probably the reflection of a screen because they're too busy staring at their phone to notice somebody checking them out.

Stop calling every girl, "bitch." You're an idiot if you think girls like that, just like you're an idiot for wearing sunglasses inside a bar.

It's gonna suck when you're 37,
still taking Molly, and going to EDM
festivals because you never tried to
do anything else with your life.

You shouldn't be annoyed if a homeless man asks you for money, you should be upset if he doesn't — because it means your outfit looks fucking cheap.

I want a girl with long, natural hair
who looks like she'd fucking kill me.
Like, she's clearly patient, but testing
her patience is sketchy.

Hey, guess what — Mondays don't suck if you go to bed at a decent hour, eat breakfast, and get a job you actually fucking like. Weird, huh?

"Live each day like it's your last."
That's the worst fucking advice ever.
That's how you end up dead, in debt,
or incarcerated.

Physical attention isn't everything.
Whether it is acknowledged or not,
intelligence will take you places in life —
places that are far more rewarding than
somebody else's bedroom.

I want a girl who's nice, but
doesn't take shit. Like, she'll cook
you dinner — but if you don't ask
politely — she'll fucking poison it.

Stop complaining about "leg day" and just be grateful you can walk. There are sharks in the ocean wishing they had a fucking "leg day."

It's Friday, you want to party with your friends tonight, but what if your dog has a nice evening planned? Did you even think about that?

Your baggage is garbage — recycle it.
Take the emotional trash of your past
and use it to create something better,
you jaded motherfucker.

The next time you meet someone who
claims they're "not a dog person,"
report them to the authorities.
Because they're probably a terrorist.

If I were a girl, I'd wear a plastic rain poncho to the bar and be like, "Stop showering me with compliments, you're getting my outfit wet!"

If you kiss a stranger at the bar, make them buy you a drink after. Because alcohol kills germs — and you probably just kissed someone filthy.

You know that feeling you get when somebody gives you advice you didn't ask for? That's how girls feel when you send a picture of your dick.

This Halloween, be the opposite of
yourself. Put on clean clothes, maybe
wash your hair — your costume:
"Someone with their shit together."

I want a girl who's smart, and knows where she's going in life. You know, like Google Maps, but with human skin, and body parts, and stuff.

Be accepting of who you are, but aspirational about who you want to be. None of this "fake it 'til you make it" bullshit — instead: Be shit 'til you're the shit.

Sunday nights are good nights to sit back, relax, and think about all the shit you needed to (but didn't) get done over the weekend.

Just once I'd like to meet a pit bull owner who will admit their dog is a total dickhead. They can't all be misunderstood, little angels.

"Fifty Shades of Grey" is just a remake of "Halloween." Stalking, mystery, playing hard to get — it's Michael Myers with a job and a helicopter.

Never apologize for something that once made you happy. If you eat someone's lunch from the office fridge, admit to it, but don't say you're sorry.

I want a girl who's tough, but caring.
Like, if I come home drunk, she'll
help me take my shoes off, but I'm
sleeping on the fucking couch.

Have good conversations. It's more rewarding to get in someone's head than it is to get in someone's pants. And, you won't get pregnant.

Vaping is a great hobby for people who already suck at other things in life, but aren't ready to commit to a career that involves sucking things for money.

If you're lonely in bed, close your eyes and imagine you're covered in lava. That's how it feels to sleep while cuddling. You're better off alone.

HALLOWEEN

Imagine a haunted house made entirely
of photos of the people you've dated.
Because your entire dating life has
been a fucking nightmare.

I often Google pictures of STDs.
Not because I think I have one, but
because I like being the friend
everyone goes to for advice.

Do sharks complain about Monday? No.
They're up early, biting stuff, chasing
shit, and being scary — reminding
everyone they're a fucking shark.

Every day, look in the mirror and say,
"I will never be this dumb again." Then,
force yourself to learn something new in
order to make it true. Repeat this each
morning and you'll find that your life and
conversations become far less boring.

You know what keeps me up at night? Dinosaurs. I mean, modern medicine and WiFi is cool and all, but we straight up missed out on birds that were 30 feet tall. That fucking sucks, man.

Just because somebody is doing better than you doesn't mean they are better than you. Unless you're an asshole; in that case, karma is just doing its fucking thing.

I want a girl who's not afraid to chase
her dreams — no matter what. Like,
even though she's wearing heels,
she'll fucking run to pet a dog.

How do we create world peace?
Two words: Oreo milkshakes.
Nobody can resist, and nobody
can fight with a brain freeze.

Spiders have the life. They don't pay rent — and they basically just hang out in a fucking hammock all day waiting for food to land in their bed.

Growing up means you stop doing
things just to annoy people — you do
things because you enjoy them. And
if that annoys people, it's a bonus.

Loyalty is tested when an experience
accidentally becomes evidence.

Dwelling on the past prevents you from kicking ass in the future. That's like looking back on summer for ideas on how to dress for winter. Focus on today, take off your fucking sandals, and concentrate on the shit that you currently have to handle.

You know the feeling of ultimate relief that you experience when you wake up from a bad dream? That's straight up how I feel after conversations with some people.

I love girls with those sharp, Freddy Krueger fingernails. They look sexy, and I know she'll never ask me to take her bowling.

Hey dudes, if a girl follows you on Instagram, it doesn't mean she wants to fuck you. Stop being a creep — she just thinks you have a cute dog.

Life is like a do-it-yourself frozen yogurt shop: It's your fault if you end up with a cup of shit that even sprinkles can't fucking fix.

Some personalities play well together,
other personalities challenge you in
ways that make you better, and, well,
a lot of personalities are best when
they're simply avoided altogether.

Sometimes I use the ATM in Spanish
just to challenge myself.

I want a girl who can carry a
conversation, and a large shovel.
That's the ideal road trip companion:
good at talking — and hiding evidence.

I've never met a nacho plate
I didn't want to impregnate.

If you're not fucking happy, maybe
instead of eliminating food, you
should consider eliminating friends.
Losers are more toxic than gluten.

Hiding your true identity from
co-workers requires fucking skills.
If you've kept the same job for over
a year, you're fucking Batman.

Girls love peanut butter. Dab a little behind your ears before you go out tonight. The best cologne has two varieties: crunchy or smooth.

Cats are like people: they're not all bad. It's just that the shitty ones get most of the attention.

THANKSGIVING

Today, be thankful you don't have
Snooki as your mom, Taylor Swift as
your ex-girlfriend, or Bill Cosby as
your grandpa.

Embrace failure. Doing so will only make you better. Now, what is meant by that is: Learn from your losses. Don't take it literally and go hug your disastrous ex or some shit.

"She's way too hot — why is she with him?" I don't know, maybe he actually has a fucking job, life goals, and doesn't live with his mom.

If you can't roast each other and
love each other simultaneously, then
you're taking your serious relationship
too fucking seriously.

Dogs can smell fear, but do you know what else they can smell? Bullshit. If your dog doesn't like somebody, it's because that person is a fucking loser.

It's called a selfie stick because if you're seen using one, you can pretty much guarantee you'll be alone your entire life.

I'm pretty sure the 11th Commandment said something about not sliding into her DMs like a fuckboy, but Moses ran out of room on the tablets.

You know that feeling you get when
you're embarrassed for someone?
That's how I feel at the zoo, as I whisper,
"You used to be King of the Jungle..."

Never blame alcohol for your bad
decisions. If you decide to tell somebody
you love them, don't you fucking dare
blame it on being drunk.

In Ancient Greece, the prostitutes were easy to find because they wore blonde wigs. I guess you could say those blondes were having more fun.

A girl once told me she wouldn't go out with me again because I drink too much. I said, "h,hjj." Then, I apologized for drunk texting her.

Ladies, a bit of advice before you
go out tonight: Never trust a man in
cargo shorts. Because chances are,
with more pockets than fingers, he's
definitely hiding something.

I love women who eat leftovers,
because there is seriously nothing
sexier than a woman determined
enough to finish what she has started.

Sure, hangovers suck, but not as
bad as listening to somebody sober
tell you about their crazy night at
Applebee's that ended at 8:00 P.M.

Money can't buy happiness, but it can buy the loud, drunk girl at the bar a taxi so she'll fucking leave. Which is basically the same thing.

You can't even tell who has money these days. You could be sitting next to some dude who is worth $44 million because he invented some app that helps your dog pick pajamas.

If you want to rid your life of dishonesty, maybe you can start by unfollowing "influencers" who are paid to straight up fucking lie to you about products they don't use from companies they don't know shit about.

Personality over possessions. Because nobody cares about the sneakers you're wearing or the handbag you're carrying when you're as vapid as the now-empty box that shit arrived in.

If you die in the hood, your homies will pour a forty. If you die in Orange County, your yoga classmates will pour a Pumpkin Spice Latte.

Your boyfriend might as well be an ice cream cone: He's cheap, he's soft — and if things get heated — he has a fucking meltdown.

I like my coffee like my weather:
none of that silly ice and shit.

Forget about finding somebody who
checks all of the boxes on a list;
focus on keeping somebody who
reality-checks all of your bullshit.

You should travel more, because
it helps you discover things about
yourself. Who knows, maybe you'll
even get lucky and find your real dad.

Don't give your kid a freaky-fucking name like Damien. You might as well name your child "Lucifer's Pen Pal." Because you know that little shit will be talking with Satan years before he talks to a girl.

Being open-minded is great — but
if you don't occasionally create AND
stick to your own beliefs — your open
mind becomes an open invitation for
others' dumb opinions.

Find someone who's both spiritual and sexual. You know, somebody who's in touch with the Universe's vibrations and shit, but somebody who will also try weird things involving your dick or tits.

At night, take comfort in knowing someone, somewhere, is thinking about you. Probably about why you suck, but hey, the thought still counts.

Have friends outside of your relationship. Sure, you might think they're the only person you need now, but have you ever moved an entire apartment with only two people? It fucking blows.

Telling someone you miss your ex, is like saying, "I miss wearing diapers." Stop missing things that were full of shit and move on.

My grandma once said, "Nothing worth having comes easy," so I showed her the Domino's Pizza app on my phone and blew her fucking mind.

Giving someone a puppy for Christmas
is a horrible idea. "Hey, I noticed
your life was lacking attachment and
responsibility. Well, here you go."

CHRISTMAS

If you must know, I prefer to use
Xmas instead of Christmas —
because I like to think of my Jesus
as a member of the X-Men.

Don't attend your high school reunion. You already avoid those people on Facebook, why would you want to see them in person?

"I only fuck with ambitious women."
Well, no shit. Because you've been
working on that mixtape for six years
and you need someone to pay your rent.

When I was a kid, we didn't have the internet. You had to have balls and tell someone they sucked right to their face.

Day drinking is done for pleasure;
night drinking is done to forget
the day. (This is why you fucking
love brunch so much.)

Never settle for less than you deserve. Don't date fucking losers, don't work a job you hate, and don't ever choose a cat instead of a dog.

As you begin thinking of New Year's resolutions, instead of thinking of all you're doing wrong, think of something you're already doing well. Then, commit to doing it just a little bit better. For example: You're already great at being single — try doing it with less complaining.

ABOUT THE AUTHOR

Writer. Creator. Instigator. Not your dad.

@SGRSTK